POEMS AND SONGS GIVEN TO ME BY GOD

Rosalie Nuttall Brown

ISBN 979-8-88644-188-8 (Paperback)
ISBN 979-8-88644-189-5 (Digital)

Covenant Books
11661 Hwy 707
Murrells Inlet, SC 29576
www.covenantbooks.com

Dedicated to my children with all my love—
Paul, David, Tommy, Deena, Deana Leigh.

And they said, "Believe on the Lord Jesus Christ,
and thou shalt be saved, and thy house."

—Acts 16:31 (KJV)

CONTENTS

ACKNOWLEDGMENTS

First and foremost, I thank God above all else for the talent He's given me.

May 1964

My first son was diagnosed with cerebral palsy.

THIS CHILD OF MINE

This crippled child that I love
Was sent to me from God above
As I hold him close to my heart
I know through life I have done my part
As I hold him close to my breast
His tears are quieted, he's at rest
As emotions surge through my soul
This child and I will meet the goal.

JESUS, KEEPER OF MY SOUL

Verse 1

> Jesus, keeper of my soul
> Came to earth to make me whole
> Gave His life on Calvary
> From my sins He set me free
> God's greatest sacrifice for me
> Jesus shed His blood for me

> Chorus:
> Jesus, keeper of my soul
> Jesus, keeper of my soul

Verse 2

> Jesus, keeper of my soul
> Came to earth to make others whole
> He died not only for me
> But for all others to set them free
> He'll do it for you when you ask
> Faith in Jesus is no task
> Just ask in faith and believe it so
> He'll set you free so to heaven you'll go

Chorus

Jesus, keeper of my soul
Jesus, keeper of your soul

Verse 3

Jesus, keeper of your soul
Came to earth to make you whole
Gave His life on Calvary
From your sin He'll set you free
God's greatest gift for you and me
Jesus came to set us free

Chorus

Jesus, keeper of your soul
Jesus, keeper of my soul

July 22, 2018

GOD IN THREE PERSONS

Verse 1

Holy Spirit come
Make your people whole
Fill each and everyone
Fill each precious soul

Verse 2

Thank you God our Father
For your saving grace
Prepare our hearts before you
In heaven save our place

Verse 3

Jesus our beloved Savior
Thank you for your touch
Thank you for salvation
We love you oh so much

Verse 4

God in three persons
Fulfill our hearts today

Live inside our lives
For all this we pray

Verse 5

Thank you God our Father
Thank you God the Son
Thank you Holy Spirit
Thank you Three In One

August 22, 2018

A poem God gave me when I was reading Exodus 3:13–14 (KJV).

I AM

Love me for who I am
Learn of me what you can
Believe on me and let it show
Tell of me what you know
Honor me with your voice
You have a choice
I AM THAT I AM

THE SIMPLE LIFE

I came into this simple life with all
    my cares and wants
I struggled within my soul for things I did not need
The simple life had come and gone,
    a longing filled my soul
Then the struggles of life had taken its toll
Then Jesus came into my life, and
    filled me with His love
The simple life came once again
    with a peace from above

    Thank you, Lord Jesus, for putting these wonderful words in my thoughts.

PRICE TAG

Two things we must remember;

1. We represent God in our actions, words, and attitude.
2. It is not about us!

GOD'S PROMISES

I want everything God has for me and you
Let's pray together and claim these too
For all He has promised in His Word
So we will bind together in one accord
Thank you, God, for all you've given
But most of all for our sins forgiven

While getting ready for church, God gave me this poem.

God's number seven; His perfect number.

SEVEN REASONS TO
GO TO HEAVEN

1.   The Father, Son, and Holy Ghost.
2.   All the loved ones we cherish the most.
3.   To walk together on the streets of gold.
4.   So much glory our eyes to behold.
5.   To sing praises to the King of kings.
6.   While heavenly angels wear heavenly wings.
7.   But most of all to hear God say, "Welcome home, my child. You're here to stay."

I thank God for His faithfulness and the talent He's given me.

This poem comes from my heart because I had a wonderful mother.

A MOTHER'S LOVE

A mother's love is here to stay
She shows her love in every way
A kind and gentle touch
To all it means so very much
A beautiful smile that lights her face
You feel her presence every place
We honor our mothers this day yearly
But every day tell them you love them dearly
What a mother means to me
Look around and you will see
On their knees before God for
        their family and others
THAT'S THE REASON God created mothers

To my children: Be this kind of parent God intended you to be.

My father was so kind to our family, never met a stranger, and anyone who entered our home was given a meal and his friendship. My father was very special to me.

AN HONOR TO FATHERS EVERYWHERE

A father is someone to look up to
        for his many examples
His life may seem rough or sometimes very simple
A loving arm around us when we are hurting
Maybe a kiss on the cheek or a word of praise
Fathers come in all shapes and sizes
But their hearts burst in pride as each
        of his children are born
His caring for us lasts our lifetime
It's because he loves God and wants
        to lead by example
He is the very one God chose for your
        family to love and cherish
As our heavenly Father wraps His arms around us
So our earthly fathers have loving arms
        to wrap around their children.

THE UNLOVABLE ONE

I thank you God for the Holy
Spirit that's been given
For Jesus your Son and my sins forgiven
For making me completely whole
For your Son Jesus and saving my soul
You knew me from the beginning
And for loving me through all my sinning
But most of all you loved me enough
to send your only begotten Son
To die on the cross for this unlovable one
Now I can sing a new song in my heart
For the family of God is what sets me apart

FAITH, HOPE, CHARITY

F-faithful
A-always
I-instruct
T-their
H-household

H-hope
O-opens
P-people
E-enter

L-love
O-opens
V-various
E-effects

G-God's
R-redemption
A-at
C-Christ's
E-existence

First Corinthians 13, it's called the love chapter.

"And now abideth faith, hope, charity, these three; but the greatest of these is Charity" (1 Corinthians 13:13).

Charity means love.

C-Christ
H-has
A-a
R-redeeming
I-innocence
T-toward
Y-you

REJOICE

Rejoice in the Lord, always; and again, I say, rejoice.

R-rejoice
E-everyone
J-Jesus
O-often
I-invites
C-Christians
E-everywhere

In church, when Pastor was preaching in Philippians
4:4–8, God gave me this thought.

JESUS IS THE MIRACLE

It takes a miracle to turn a life around
It takes a miracle to save a soul
Jesus is the miracle
God sent to you and me
It took a miracle, when we were found

Chorus:
Jesus is the miracle
He died for you and me, He loved
    us so to die on Calvary!

God gave a miracle in His only Son
He gave it all, to turn our life around
He loves the work that He's begun
It took a miracle in our life He found

Chorus:
Jesus is the miracle
He died for you and me, He loved
    us so to die on Calvary!
Jesus is the miracle
He died for you and me, He loved
    us so to die on Calvary!

THANK YOU, GOD

Thank you, God, for the talent you've given me
For Jesus who died to set me free
For your loving arms that show you care.
For setting me free from my sin and despair
Thank you for my poems and songs
That put joy in my heart and freedom from wrongs
Let me be a beacon of your life
Keep me always from sin and strife

MY LIFE IN YOU

My life is set in stone
I feel so all alone,
Day by day I go along
Where's my joy? Where's my song?
I get down on my knees to pray
This is where I need to stay
God, return the joy to my soul
This is my love for you, my goal.

TURMOIL WITHIN

Verse 1

>My life is in turmoil I can't control
>Lord, I've given you my heart and soul
>The things that come against me
>   are from deep within
>Send me the joy and peace of
>   your love once again

Verse 2

>I'm your child and always will be
>I have the love of Jesus deep within me
>I release this burden to you right now
>I can feel your arms about me
>Even though I can't see how

Thank you, my Lord and Savior, for the peace that passes all understanding.

>And the peace of God, which passeth all
>   understanding, shall keep your hearts
>   and minds through Christ Jesus.
>   —Philippians 4:7

HOLY SPIRIT, COME

Holy Spirit, come, fill me with your love
Wrap me in your arms; send your peace from above
Thank you, God, Omnificent
For Jesus whom you sent
To die on the cross of Calvary
To save lost souls like me

November 30, 2020, my beloved husband went to
be with Jesus.

He was a faithful and loving man.
God took away his suffering.
I'll meet him again in heaven.

HIS ARMS

I miss his love and his arms around me
But God in His faithfulness stepped in
Now I rely on His arms around me
To free me and keep me from sin
One of these days I will see him again
We will be known as we were known
Free from shame and sin
When I step into the loving arms of Jesus alone

LOST SONG

I lost the song in my heart since my husband died
I sat around for months and cried
Why did he have to go and leave me alone?
My heart cries out in a pitiful moan
I know he's with God in heaven at last
I'll see him again when my journey is past

PEACE

I love you Lord and will forever
The peace you bring from up above
Sent down from above, from you
Makes me know in my heart
Your love for me is true

MY SONG

I found my song again today,
God sent it to me without delay.
It's the song "It Is Well with My Soul"
Praying for answers, I met my goal
As I sing this wonderful song today,
I know my Redeemer lives in my heart to stay.

Thank you, sweet Jesus
It is well with my soul.

PRAYERFULNESS

I've got to read my Bible and pray
That's the most important thing today
I go to church to worship God
He knows my presence on this sod
One day I will meet Jesus in heaven above
For now I render to His love.
His faithfulness keeps me strong
He keeps me from doing wrong
I want to serve Him with all my heart
To make heaven my home and never to part

Thank you, God, for the talent you've given me.

LOVING GOD

I love God who gave me life
I love the Savior Jesus who saved my life
I love the God who He is to me
I love Jesus for all He does, you see
God does this for all the world
Jesus died for us because He is Lord
You are my life God
Jesus gave us life from all our strife
He gave His life on Calvary
Then sent the Holy Spirit to live within me

REVIVAL

We've been in revival and it's plain to see
God still has a plan for me
I questioned my purpose since my
      husband has been gone
Some days I feel so all alone
Surrounded by family and loved ones all the time
My life still has no rhythm or rhyme
I gave it all to God one night
I felt His presence in the morning light
He spoke to me that I have a choice
Be His light in the world and just rejoice

TAKE A LOOK

It's a book, it's a book
Take a look, take a look
It's a Bible I see
It's a Bible for me
It tells me of Jesus
And how He loves me
It's the good book I see
Take a look
Take a look

MY REDEEMER LIVETH

I know my redeemer liveth to make
    intercession for me
He died a cruel death on the cross of Calvary
He buried my sins under His blood
My tears flowed down as a flood
He made a new person out of me
He's given me joy, He set me free
I'll praise Him as long as I live
My heart, my soul, to Him I give

I AM SORRY

I am so stretched out; I feel I am lost within myself
Dear God I need your help
Saying I'm sorry is the hardest thing that I do
But I say it simply because I love you
I mess up a lot of times it seems
But then I remember our wonderful dreams
I am Sorry
I don't want to give up on life
I know I can be a better wife

MY LIFE IS YOURS

My life is but a vapor that will soon pass away
Help me Lord to be all that you want each day
I turned over my life to you a long time ago
I'll serve you faithfully until my time to go
Here's my mind, my heart, and my soul
Thank you, Lord, for making me whole

LEAVING ME BEHIND

I didn't want you to go and break my heart
I knew we'd be together and never part
But God had a plan for your life it seems
Which shattered my heart and left only dreams
I know someday we'll be together again
Just wait for me Darling as I enter in
It seems so long ago you left me
But one day I'll join you and you will see
The heavens will ring on this glorious day
When in your arms I'll forever stay
Jesus had a purpose for your life
I struggled within not being your wife
I loved you then and always will
Just wait for me Darling while I remain here, still

GOD, MY SHEPHERD

The Lord is my Shepherd
He dried my tears, my prayers He heard
I have no wants, He meets my needs
He calms my soul, He sets my goal
He restores me throughout the night
The next day all is right
I fear not death or the harms
I'm secure and safe in my Savior's arms
I can eat my fill at my Master's table
My head He anoints from a ladle
Goodness and mercy are my friends
They follow me all my life
I dwell with Jesus and am free from sin and strife

ME, A BEACON

Lord help me to be a beacon for thee
Open my eyes that I might see
Use my lips to tell of your love
Of the goodness you've sent to me from above
The hands you made for me to hug others
Family members for starts, especially our mothers
Our feet to spread the good Word around
No matter where we are at, we are not bound
Our whole body as a vessel for you
Help me always to stay true

MAINLAND

Following the seacoast with my son
My heart explodes, so much fun
Seeing lighthouses one by one
Fall trees glistening in the sun
Thank you, God, for your majestic beauty
All the places I get to see

SITES TO SEE

A moose, a moose, on the loose
Turkeys, turkeys here and there
On the side roads everywhere
On New Hampshire's scenic route
Seeing these how we shout
Seeing mountains, rivers, and streams
How majestic from God above
Shown to us with His love

PRAISES TO GOD

Thank you, God, for the hills and valleys
For the life you've given me
For the family you've blessed me with
And all the years beyond me to see
You've granted me a good life
Helped me through my sorrows and strife
My heart, mind, body, and soul I freely give to thee
I'll live my life prayerfully
And to you, dear God, I'll be true

SON OF GOD

Son of God, to Calvary He trod
Beaten and scourged
Weeping was heard
A thorny Crown
A life laid down
For my sins and yours
Our lives He adores
So one day when we walk
And with Jesus we talk
Free from all sin
Peace and joy within
Loved ones we see
And forever to be
With Jesus above
Because of His love
Our sins He did bear
His love He did share
Thank you, Jesus, for saving my soul
Until I meet you in heaven
This is my goal
To live my life forever
Sin-free

HOMECOMING

So much beauty for me to behold
As I meet Jesus on a street of gold
Loved ones, friends, and people everywhere
So much to see as I walk here and there
Thank you, Jesus, Thank you, God
It's been a long journey that I've trod
Sins forgiven, under the blood
No more tears, flowing like a flood
Jesus says, "You're free from sin"
Welcome home, child, enter in
Beauty, beauty everywhere
I'm so glad I made it here

HOLY SPIRIT

Holy Spirit, shine your light on me
Help me keep my vessel full
Guide me always to do right
To always remain in your sight
Direct my path every day
Teach my heart to do what's right
Father, Son, Holy Ghost
The three in one, I love the most
Before all others you will be
My heart's desire you shall see
Daily praise I send your way
In my heart is where you'll stay
Thank you for all you do
To the three of you, I'll be true

NEW DAY DAWNS

A new day dawns on the way home
A lot more of this world I'd like to see
But to be in the arms of Jesus
Is where I'd rather be
My eyes will be opened to everything around
As I walk the holy ground
Streets of gold I shall behold
But to behold Jesus on the streets of gold
Loved ones and friends here and there
And spending eternity with Jesus
As He greets us and says well done

TOUCHING JESUS

I can get in touch with Jesus every day
As I get down on my knees to pray
One day though I will see Him
To touch His nail-scarred hands
And sing praises as a hymn
Jesus is alive!
I will survive

THE ANCHOR

Jesus, anchor of my soul
To reach heaven is my goal
Keeping myself from sin and shame
Daily prayers and praise are my aim
Keeping my thoughts on heaven above
Finding solace in His love
To hear Him say well done now rest
Knowing I gave Him all my best

SACRIFICIAL LAMB

The sacrificial Lamb
I'm glad you came
To set me free
I'm no longer lame
You are God in three persons
God the Father
God the Son
God the Holy Spirit
The three in one
I worship you for who you are
You are never far away
Just a whispered prayer
Is all I have to say

TALENTS

God, you've given me many talents
And I praise you Lord for these gifts
When the words come flowing through me
My heart and soul just lifts
I want to invest in all of these
Your love and you Lord to please
I'm glad you have given me all of this
My talents I don't want to miss
Help me never to refuse
The talents you've given me to use

THANK YOU, JESUS

Jesus saves and sets us free
He does this for you and me
When I go to bed to rest
I pray to God, I've done my best
He hears every prayer request
And He's happy we passed the test
I am His and He is mine
He embraces us with love divine
Jesus thank you for all of this
I want heaven as my home
This is one thing, I don't want to miss
Jesus, I am yours and you are mine
Help me always let my light shine

FORGIVENESS

Forgiveness comes from God above
Sent to us with His great love
Jesus died for you and me
On the cross at Calvary
God's only Son sent so we may live
He gave His life for our sins to forgive
Forgiveness comes to you and me
Jesus came to set us free
A whispered prayer in the early light
His arms around us in the night

THE FLAG

The flag stands for freedom, given to you and me
It stands for our nation and our liberty
For me it stands for so much more
Look and you will see
The blue for the sky, the stars to brighten our way
The red for the blood He shed, the white for purity
It's a symbol of God's love for us
As it flies majestically
Thank you, God, for reminding me
Of your majesty

PRAYER

The Son of God looks down on me
He knows my thoughts, my heart He can see
I always want my thoughts clean and pure
So I can make heaven my home for sure
When I stay on my knees and pray
My heart can stay pure for another day
It takes prayer and good thoughts in order to stay
A person pleasing to God in every way

I LIVE IN YOU

I live in you; Christ tells us all
Who gives their hearts to Him
I will keep you so you won't fall
Take my hand and you shall live
I touched His nail-scarred hand
And I felt His very heart beat
To you, I finally of myself give
Every part of my life to you, I live

CRUISING WITH GOD

On a cruise with my son-in-law and daughter
I felt the cool breeze coming off of the water
God keep us safe as we travel each day
A new port to visit, a new place to stay
Show me your will in all that I do
Keep me faithful as I travel with you
Keep me safe as each place I ponder
Knowing one day I'll see you up yonder
Keep my feet planted on solid ground
Until I hear the great trumpet sound

THE CHOICE

A tiny voice from within
Keeps me free from sin
It tells me of my Father's love
Sent from heaven above
He speaks in a still small voice
And says I have a choice
I can live each day for Him
And win my family
So we can all rejoice around the throne
When He says, "Come on in"
With His majestic tone

TEARS

I cry and cry but I don't know why
As each day goes by and by
I guess because I miss you so
As on life's path I go
It's been a year since you've been gone
And I feel so all alone
The tears won't stop as I question God
But the answer never comes
As in this life I trod
I know you're free from suffering
And in heaven you're at peace
I just wait on God for my release
As I continue life down here
Until God calls me to my home up there

JESUS CARES

Jesus came to me in the night
And said He'd done His part
I answered Him with a prayer
And gave to Him my heart
He came that way in a still small voice
And said I had a choice
To serve Him every day
And love Him the same way
"I will, Lord Jesus," was my reply
With all my heart I will try
He said, "It's all I can ask"
Leave all your sins in the past

GOD'S FAITHFULNESS

God you are so faithful
I love you for all this
You gave Jesus to die for all
So heaven we won't miss
I pray that I can live for you
And always to you be true
If I falter on my path
As I walk this earth below
Shelter me in your arms
As I continue to grow
I need your strength to carry on
Until life down here is gone

JESUS

Come meek and lowly
God's special Child
Come as our Savior
So quiet and mild
God sent us this Child
For all to be reconciled
To all that He loved
Saved by Jesus, the beloved
Call out to Him today
Jesus is the only way
Salvation He'll bring to you
He'll guide you in all you do
Be faithful all the way
Pray to Jesus every day

GIFTS FOR JESUS

My life to Him I give as long as I live
My voice to sing praises to Him
My love for Him I bring
My feet to spread the good news
For others to receive and use
My heart in praises to sing
My best to Him I bring
My hands I raise in worship
As praises flow from my lip
My heart and soul I give you
In everything I say or do

GOD'S MERCY

The mercies of God reach beyond our sins
As we are cleansed in our hearts within
They are new every day
As we worship and pray
Set free by the blood of the Lamb
Who is the great I Am
My hand I raise in worship
As praises flow from my lip

THE ALPHABET OF GOD

King James Version

A.   Almighty—Alpha

He is the Almighty God.

> "I am Alpha and Omega, the beginning and the ending, saith the Lord, which is; and which was; and which is to come, the Almighty" (Revelation 1:8).

B.   Beloved Savior—Blessed One

> "And lo a voice from heaven, saying, This is my beloved Son, in whom I am well pleased" (Matthew 3:17).

C. Creator

> "In the beginning God cre-
> ated the heaven and the earth"
> (Genesis 1:1).

> "Thou art worthy, O Lord,
> to receive glory and honor and
> power: for thou hast created all
> things, for thy pleasure they are
> and were created" (Revelation
> 4:11).

D. Deity—Deliverer

Supreme Being as per *Webster's Dictionary*:

> "*There shall come out of Zion
> the deliverer*" (Romans 11:26).

> "The *righteous* cry, and the
> Lord heareth, and delivereth
> them out of all their troubles"
> (Psalms 34:17).

E. Everlasting—Eternal

> Abraham called the name of the Lord, the
> Everlasting God.

"Before the mountains were brought forth, or ever thou hadst formed the earth and the world, even from everlasting to everlasting, thou *art* God" (Psalm 90:2).

"The eternal God *is thy* refuge, and underneath *are* the everlasting arms" (Deuteronomy 33:27).

F. Father—Our Father
    Matthew 6:9–13 says:

> After this manner therefore pray ye: Our Father which art in heaven, Hallowed be thy name.
> Thy kingdom come. Thy will be done in earth, as *it is* in heaven. Give us this day our daily bread.
> And forgive us our debts, as we forgive our debtors.
> And lead us not into temptation, but deliver us form evil: For thine is the kingdom, and the power, and the glory, for ever, Amen.

F. Faithful

> "God *is* faithful, by whom ye were called unto the fellowship of His Son Jesus Christ our Lord" (1 Corinthians 1:9).

G. Guide

> God in three persons—Father, Son, Holy Ghost.

> "For this God *is* our God for ever and ever: he will be our guide *even* unto death" (Psalms 48:14).

H. Healer

> "Who forgiveth all thine iniquities; who healeth all thy diseases" (Psalms 103:3).

> "Heal me, O Lord, and I shall be healed; save me, and I shall be saved: for thou *art* my praise" (Jeremiah 17:14).

> "But he *was* wounded for our transgressions, he *was* bruised for our iniquities: the chastise-

ment of our peace *was* upon him; and with his stripes we are healed" (Isaiah 53:5).

I.

I Am

"And God said unto Moses, I Am that I Am: and he said, Thus shalt thou say unto the children of Israel, I Am hath sent me unto you" (Exodus 3:14).

J.   Jehovah

Jehovah means God.

"Speak thou also unto the children of Israel, saying, Verily my Sabbaths ye shall keep: for it *is* a sign between me and you throughout your generations; that *ye* may know that I *am* the Lord that doth sanctify you" (Exodus 31:13).

Judge

"Before the Lord: for he cometh to judge the earth: he

shall judge the world with righteousness, and the people with
his truth" (Psalms 96:13).

"*I am* he that liveth, and
was dead; and, behold, I am alive
for ever more, Amen; and have
the keys of hell and of death"
(Revelation 1:18).

"And the heavens shall
declare his righteousness: for God
is judge himself" Selah (Psalms
50:6).

K. King of Kings

"And the Lord shall be king
over all the earth: in that day shall
there be one LORD, and his name
one" (Zechariah 14:9).

"Which in his times he shall
show, *who is* the blessed and only
Potentate, the King of kings, and
Lord of lords" (1 Timothy 6:15).

L. Lord of Lords

"And he hath on *his* vesture
and on his thigh a name written,

King of kings, and Lord of
lords" (Revelation 19:16).

Romans 10:9–13.

M.   Majesty

"Mighty King, Master of
everything" (Hebrews 1:1–10).

N.   Nobility

"And he hath on his vesture
and on his thigh a name written,
King of kings, and Lord of
lords" Revelation 19:16.

"And Pilate wrote a title,
and put *it* on the cross. And the
writing was, Jesus of Nazareth
the King of the Jews" (John
19:19).

O.   Omnipotent

"Alleluia: for the Lord
God omnipotent reigneth"
(Revelation 19:6).

P.   Prince of Peace

> "For unto us a child is born, unto us a son is given: and the government shall be upon his shoulder: and his name shall be called Wonderful, Counselor, The Mighty God, The everlasting Father, The Prince of Peace" (Isaiah 9:6).

Q.   Quietness

> "And the work of righteousness shall be peace; and the effect of righteousness quietness and assurance for ever" (Isaiah 32:17).

> "And after the earthquake a fire: but the LORD was not in the fire: and after the fire a still small voice" (1 Kings 19:12).

R.   Restorer

> "He restoreth my soul" (Psalms 23:3).

S. Savior

> "For therefore we both labor and suffer reproach, because we trust in the living God, who is Savior of all men, specially of those that believe" (1 Timothy 4:10).

T. Truth

> "Jesus saith unto him, I am the way, the truth, and the life: no man cometh unto the Father but by me" (John 14:6).

U. Unity

> "So we, *being* many, are one body in Christ, and every one members one of another" (Romans 12:5).

V. Victory

> "For whatsoever is born of God overcometh the world: and this is the victory that overcometh the world *even* our faith" (1 John 5:4).

W.   Wonderful

> "O Lᴏʀᴅ, thou *art* my God;
> I will exalt thee, I will praise thy
> name; for thou hast done won-
> derful *things, thy* counsels of old
> *are* faithfulness *and* truth" (Isaiah
> 25:1).

X.   X-MAS

Christmas is *Jesus's birthday.* Some people use an "X" then "Mas"—*don't* let an "X" take Christ out of your life!

Y. Yoke

> "For my yoke *is* easy, and
> my burden is light" (Matthew
> 11:30).

Z.   Zealous

> "For the zeal of thine house
> hath eaten me up" (Psalms 69:9).

> "For I bear them record
> that they have a zeal of God, but
> not according to knowledge"
> (Romans 10:2).

ABOUT THE AUTHOR

Rosalie Nuttall Brown grew up in Latrobe, Pennsylvania. She moved to Missouri in the '60s at the age of twenty-one with her family. She is the youngest of seventeen siblings. She is the mother of four grown children and now has seventeen grandchildren and thirty-two great-grandchildren. She was a nurse for thirty years and retired in 2014. She plays the guitar on Sundays and Wednesdays at church and the keyboard at home. She loves to go camping and fishing.

www.ingramcontent.com/pod-product-compliance
Lightning Source LLC
Chambersburg PA
CBHW031407160726
47993CB00003B/1138